W9-BYZ-265

On the cover:

The **bobcat** is the most common wildcat in North America. It got its name from its short bobbed tail. These wildcats are a little bigger than house cats and can see and hear very well. They are very shy and won't come near people.

A Reading/Language Arts Program

Program Authors

Diane August
Donald R. Bear
Janice A. Dole
Jana Echevarria
Douglas Fisher
David Francis
Vicki Gibson
Jan E. Hasbrouck
Scott G. Paris
Timothy Shanahan
Josefina V. Tinajero

Macmillan/McGraw-Hill

Contributors

Time Magazine, Accelerated Reader

RFB&D
learning through listening

Students with print disabilities may be eligible to obtain an accessible, audio version of the pupil edition of this textbook. Please call Recording for the Blind & Dyslexic at 1-800-221-4792 for complete information.

B

The McGraw·Hill Companies

Macmillan/McGraw-Hill

Published by Macmillan/McGraw-Hill, of McGraw-Hill Education, a division of The McGraw-Hill Companies, Inc., Two Penn Plaza, New York, New York 10121.

Printed in the United States of America

ISBN: 978-0-02-199962-0/1, Bk. 2

MHID: 0-02-199962-7/1, Bk. 2

3 4 5 6 7 8 9 (027/055) 12 11 10 09

Welcome to
California *Treasures*

Imagine having a pet dinosaur who wants to go to school, learning about how *real* animals act as teams, or reading about a kitten who thinks the moon is a bowl of milk. Your **Student Book** contains these and other award-winning fiction and nonfiction selections.

Treasures Meets California Standards

The instruction provided with each reading selection in your **Student Book** will ensure that you meet all the **California Reading/Language Arts Standards** for your grade. Throughout the book, special symbols (such as ✔) and codes (such as R 1.1.2) have been added to show where and how these standards are being met. They will help you know *what* you are learning and *why*.

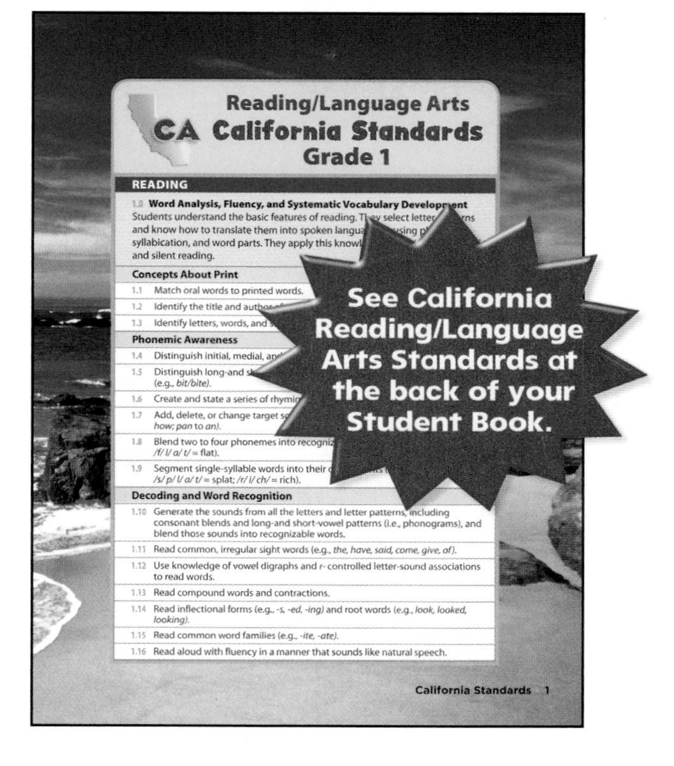

Reading/Language Arts
CA California Standards
Grade 1

READING

1.0 **Word Analysis, Fluency, and Systematic Vocabulary Development**
Students understand the basic features of reading. They select letter ... rns and know how to translate them into spoken langua... using p... syllabication, and word parts. They apply this knowl... and silent reading.

Concepts About Print

1.1 Match oral words to printed words.
1.2 Identify the title and auth...
1.3 Identify letters, words, and s...

Phonemic Awareness

1.4 Distinguish initial, medial, an...
1.5 Distinguish long-and s... (e.g., *bit/bite*).
1.6 Create and state a series of rhymin...
1.7 Add, delete, or change target s... *how; pan* to *an*).
1.8 Blend two to four phonemes into recogniz... /f/ l/ a/ t/ = flat).
1.9 Segment single-syllable words into their c... /s/ p/ l/ a/ t/ = splat; /r/ i/ ch/ = rich).

Decoding and Word Recognition

1.10 Generate the sounds from all the letters and letter patterns, including consonant blends and long-and short-vowel patterns (i.e., phonograms), and blend those sounds into recognizable words.
1.11 Read common, irregular sight words (e.g., *the, have, said, come, give, of*).
1.12 Use knowledge of vowel digraphs and *r*-controlled letter-sound associations to read words.
1.13 Read compound words and contractions.
1.14 Read inflectional forms (e.g., *-s, -ed, -ing*) and root words (e.g., *look, looked, looking*).
1.15 Read common word families (e.g., *-ite, -ate*).
1.16 Read aloud with fluency in a manner that sounds like natural speech.

California Standards 1

What do these symbols mean?

- CA = Tested Standards in California
- ✔ = Skill or Strategy that will appear on your test
- R = Reading Standards
- W = Writing Standards
- LC = Language Conventions Standards
- LAS = Listening and Speaking Standards

Macmillan/McGraw-Hill

Unit 2

History/Social Science

Our Families, Our Neighbors

THE BIG QUESTION

Theme Opener LAS 1.1.0 2

Research Activity W 1.1.0. 4

THEME: Animal Families

Talk About It LAS 1.1.0 6

Our Mom and Dad **Words to Know** R 1.1.11 8

Animal Moms and Dads **Nonfiction** R 1.2.0. . .12
by Jose Ramos

Over in the Meadow **Poetry** R 1.3.0, LAS 1.2.1. 28

Writing: **Expository (Report)** W 1.1.0, LC 1.1.2 34

THEME: Helping Out

Talk About It LAS 1.1.0 36

Who Will Help? **Words to Know** R 1.1.11 38

Little Red Hen **Folktale** R 1.2.7, R 1.3.0 42
retold by Cynthia Rothman, illustrated by David Diaz

From Wheat to Bread **Science** R 1.2.0. 58

Writing: **Expository (How-To)** W 1.1.0, LC 1.1.2 64

THEME: Our Neighborhood

Talk About It LAS 1.1.0 66

I Live Here **Words to Know** R 1.1.11 68

On the Map Nonfiction R 1.2.0 70

CA Standards Practice
The Farmers Market
History/Social Science R 1.2.0 78

Writing: **Expository (Report)** W 1.1.1, LC 1.1.2 80

THEME: At Home

Talk About It LAS 1.1.0 82

Too Big for One **Words to Know** R 1.1.11 84

The Pigs, the Wolf, and the Mud Fantasy R 1.3.1 88
by Ellen Tarlow, illustrated by Pablo Bernasconi

Homes Around the World History/Social Science R 1.2.0 106

Writing: **Narrative (Story)** W 1.2.1, LC 1.1.7 110

THEME: Neighborhood Fun

Talk About It LAS 1.1.0 112

A Show **Words to Know** R 1.1.11 114

Beth and the Band Realistic Fiction R 1.2.7 . . . 118
by Anne Miranda, illustrated by Lynne Cravath

Shake a Rattle! Performing Arts R 1.2.0 136

Writing: **Narrative (Story)** W 1.2.1, LC 1.1.6 140

STANDARDS PRACTICE: Show What You Know

Frog Lost Fiction R 1.2.0 142

Make a Book! Nonfiction R 1.2.0 144

Critical Thinking 146

Glossary 148

Unit 2
Our Families, Our Neighbors

How do families and neighbors help one another?

Theme Launcher Video

Find out more about families and neighbors at **www.macmillanmh.com**.

How do families and neighbors help one another?

Do you help people in your family? Do they help you? You may help set the table or give the dog a bath. Your mom or dad may read you a story or make your favorite snack.

Neighborhood people help, too. The crossing guard helps you cross the street. The librarian helps you pick out books. Post office workers bring your mail. A lot of people help you. And you help a lot of people, too!

Research Activities

Make a neighorhood mural. Draw neighborhood places on the mural. Then draw a person who helps you. Cut out the person. Paste your person on the mural.

Keep Track of Ideas

As you read, use the Four-Door organizer to draw and write about your family and neighbors. Draw a person and show how they help. You can include places, too.

Research Toolkit

Conduct Your Unit 2 Research Online with:

Research Roadmap
Follow step-by-step guide to complete your research project.

Online Resources

- Topic Finder and other Research Tools
- Videos and Virtual Fieldtrips
- Photos and Drawings for Presentations
- Related Articles and Web Resources

California Web Site Links

LOG ON Go to www.macmillanmh.com for more information.

California People

Alice Waters, Chef

Alice Waters is a chef who thinks it's important to use local food. She teaches children to grow food in gardens and use fresh food in cooking.

Animal Families

Talk About It

How are animal families like our families?

LOG ON Find out more about animal families at www.macmillanmh.com.

We are **two** little cats.
Our mom and dad are big cats.

This is our mom.
Look at **her** jump.

This is our dad.
He can run!

Here **they** are.
We like our mom and dad!

CA Comprehension

Genre

Nonfiction gives information about a topic.

Summarize

Main Idea and Details

Use your Main Idea and Details Web.

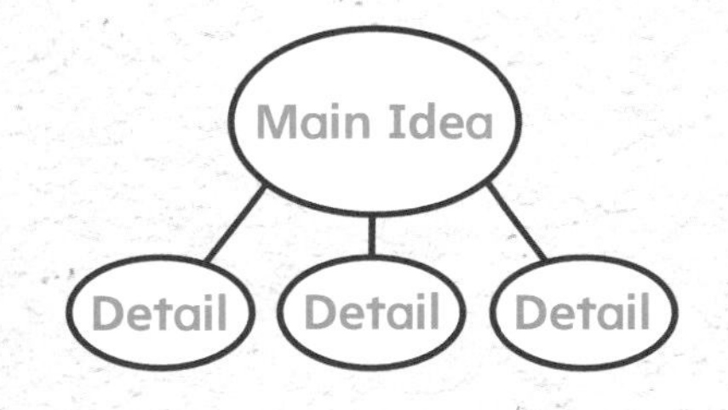

Read to Find Out

What do animal moms and dads do?

Animal Moms and Dads

by Jose Ramos

What do animal moms do?
They do a lot.

What do animal dads do?
They do a lot, too.

My mom has food.
It is good!

My dad got food, too.
Dad and I like it a lot.

My mom licks and licks.
I am clean.

My dad picks and picks.
Now I am clean.

Mom and I will hop, hop, hop.
I am in **her** sack.

My dad has a very big back.
I sit on top!

Look at **our** mom and dad.
This is a job for **two**.

We are in here.
Good job, Mom and Dad!

What can moms and dads do?

Moms and dads can play, too!

Read Together

Meet Jose Ramos

Jose Ramos says, "When I was young, my dad took me to the zoo. I wanted to take a photo of every monkey I saw! Today, I'm a dad. I take my kids to the zoo. We take pictures of our favorite animals."

CA Author's Purpose

Jose Ramos wants the reader to learn about animals. Draw an animal with its mom and dad. Write about it.

LOG ON Find out more about Jose Ramos at **www.macmillanmh.com**.

Critical Thinking

Retell the Selection

Use the Retelling Cards to retell the selection in order.

Retelling Cards

Think and Compare

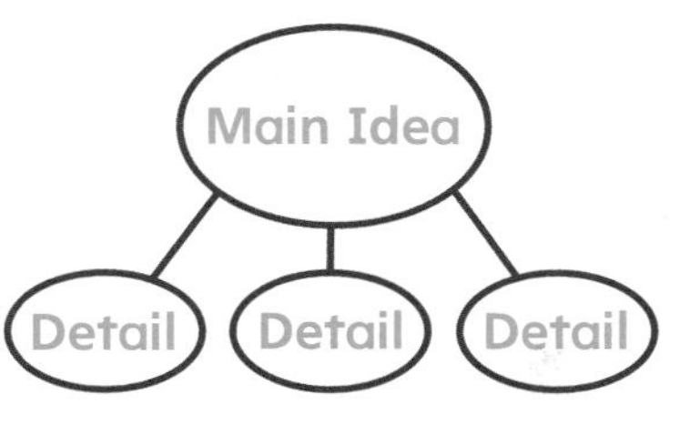

1. How do animal moms and dads take care of their babies?
2. How do the grown-ups in your family take care of you?
3. How do other animals you know take care of their babies?
4. How is *Animal Moms and Dads* like "Our Mom and Dad"? How is it different?

CA

Poetry

Genre
In a Poem, words are often put together so that they are fun to say.

Literary Element
Rhythmic Patterns are sounds and words that repeat. These give the poem a certain beat.

Find out more about animal families at www.macmillanmh.com.

Over in the Meadow

An Old Counting Rhyme

Over in the meadow,
In the sand in the sun,
Lived an old mother turtle
And her little turtle one.
"Dig," said the mother.
"I dig," said the one.
So they dug all day
In the sand in the sun.

Over in the meadow,
Where the stream runs blue,
Lived an old mother fish
and her little fishes two.

"Swim," said the mother.
"We swim," said the two.
So they swam all day
Where the stream runs blue.

Over in the meadow,
In the wide oak tree,
Lived an old mother owl
And her little owls three.
"Whoo," said the mother.
"Whoo, Whoo," said the three.
So they whooed all night
In the wide oak tree.

Critical Thinking

How are these moms and babies like the parents and babies in *Animal Moms and Dads*? How are they different?

Write About Families

Sam wrote about what some families do.

Your Turn

Think about families
you know.

Write about how families
take care of each other.

Writer's Checklist

 Does my report have a title?

 Did I write about families?

 Does each sentence have
a **noun**?

Helping Out

Talk About It

How do you help?
What jobs do you
like to do?

LOG ON Find out more about helping at www.macmillanmh.com.

Who Will Help?

Words to Know

who
no
some
of
eat

"Look at this mess," said Ben.
"**Who** will help?"

"We have **no** mops," said Jen.
"We have no bags," said Tim.

"Let's pick up," said Ben.
"I can get **some of** it," said Jen.

"I can help, too," said Tim.
"I will **eat** some!"

Comprehension

Genre

A **Folktale** is a story that has been told for many years.

Summarize

Retell

Use your Retelling Chart.

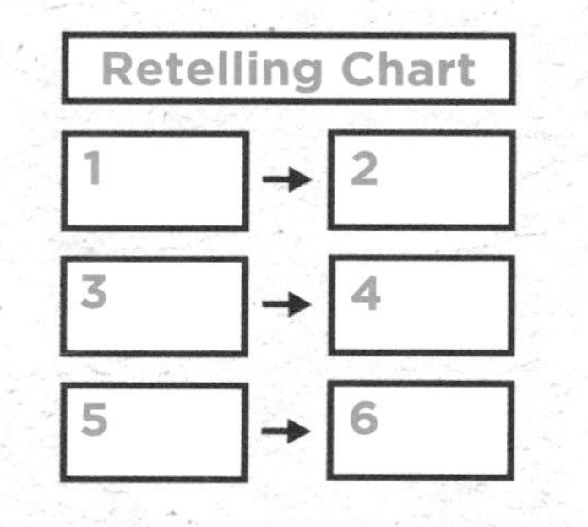

Read to Find Out

How does Little Red Hen make bread?

retold by Cynthia Rothman
illustrated by David Diaz

Award Winning Illustrator

Little Red Hen had a bit **of** wheat.
"**Who** will help plant?" asked Hen.

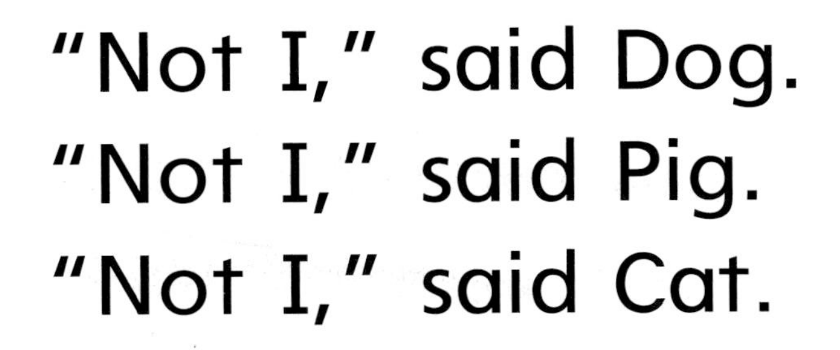

"Not I," said Dog.
"Not I," said Pig.
"Not I," said Cat.

"I will go to the well," said Hen.
"Who will help get **some** water?"

"Not I," said Cat.
"Not I," said Dog.
"Not I," said Pig.

"This is a big job," said Hen.
"Who will help get the wheat?"

"Not I," said Cat.
"Not I," said Dog.
"Not I," said Pig.

"I will mix and mix," said Hen.
"Who will help mix?"

"Not I," said Cat.
"Not I," said Dog.
"Not I," said Pig.

"Come quick!" said Hen.
"Look at this bread!"

“This is the best bread,” said Hen.
“Who will help me **eat** some?”

“Let me,” said Pig.
“Let me,” said Cat.
“Let me,” said Dog.

"**No**! No!" said Hen.
"This is a job for me!"

David Diaz's Job

David Diaz says, "I remember drawing a face on a worksheet when I was in first grade. I knew then that drawing was what I wanted to do when I grew up."

Other books by David Diaz

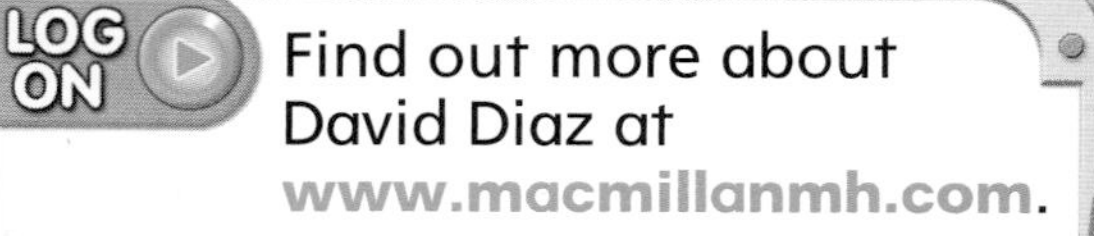

CA Illustrator's Purpose

David Diaz drew funny animals. Draw and write about one of the animals.

Critical Thinking

Retell the Story

Use the Retelling Cards to retell the story in order.

Retelling Cards

Think and Compare

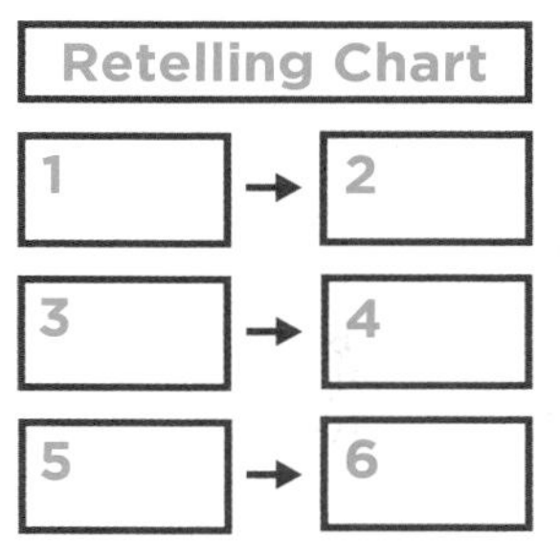

1. What does Little Red Hen do with the wheat?
2. What kind of help do you need when you make food?
3. Do you think Little Red Hen should have shared the bread? Tell why or why not.
4. How is Little Red Hen like the bears in "Who Will Help?"

Read Together

From Wheat to Bread

Science

Genre
Nonfiction gives information about a topic.

Text Feature
A Diagram is a picture that shows the parts of something.

Content Vocabulary
grow
kernels
factory

LOG ON Find out more about helping out at www.macmillanmh.com.

How does wheat **grow**?
How do we use it?

Seeds

Wheat starts as a little seed.
Farmers plant the seeds.

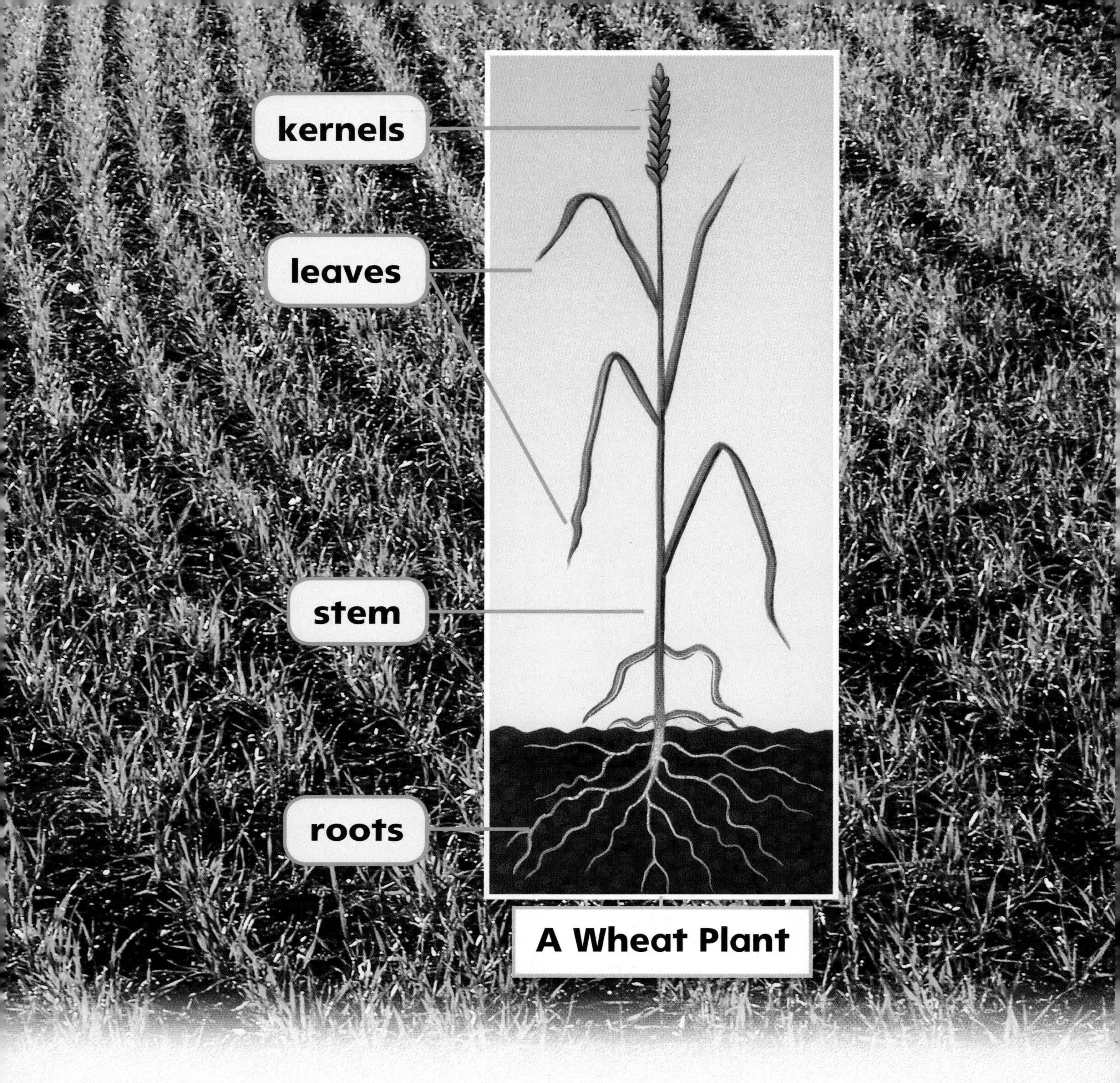

A Wheat Plant

The little plants have to get sun.
They have to get water.
They will grow to be big.

Now the wheat is tan.
The farmer picks off the **kernels**.
The kernels are good to eat.

The kernels go to a **factory**.
Here they are crushed.
The little bits of wheat are flour.

We use flour to make bread.
We use it in good things to eat.
That is what we do with wheat!

CA Critical Thinking

- Where does bread come from?
- Who helps Little Red Hen make bread?
- Who helps make bread in "From Wheat to Bread"?

How to Make a Snack

Eva wrote about how to make a snack.

Your Turn

There are many kinds of sandwiches.

Think about a sandwich you like.

Tell how to make this sandwich.

Writer's Checklist

 Are the steps in the right order?

 Do the nouns that mean more than one end with *s*?

 Does each sentence begin with a capital letter?

CA Talk About It

Where do you live? What is your neighborhood like?

LOG ON Find out more about neighborhoods at www.macmillanmh.com.

TIME FOR KIDS
Our
Neighborhood

Words to Know

live

place

many

out

I Live Here

I **live** here.
It is a big **place**.

Many kids live here, too.
We go **out** to play a lot!

Comprehension

Genre

Nonfiction

A nonfiction article gives information about a topic.

Summarize

Main Idea and Details

Look for details that show what the town is like.

On the Map

Greg and Stef **live** in a big town.

They go **out** a lot.

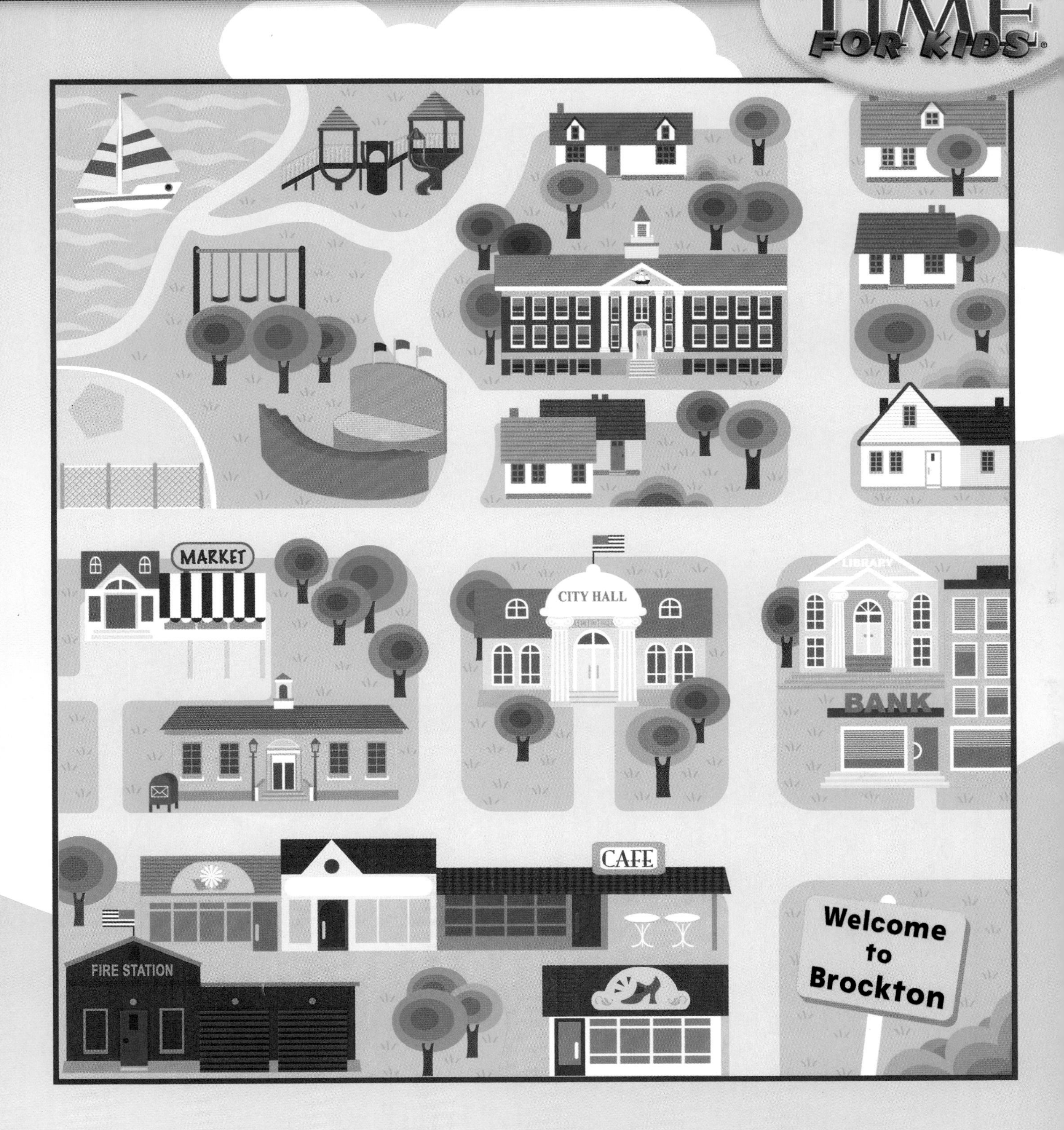

Here is the town on a map.

Greg and Stef go here a lot.
It is red. It has bricks.
It has **many** steps.
What is it?

Can you spot it on the map?

Greg and Stef like this
place a lot!
It has swings and sand.
What is it?

Can you spot it on the map?

Greg and Stef go here
to get stamps.
What is it?

Can you spot it on the map?

Critical Thinking

Tell What You Learned

What did you learn about Greg and Stef's town?

Think and Compare

1. What places in town did Greg and Stef go to?
2. What places do you like to go to in your town?
3. What places would you put on a map of your town?
4. How are the places in "I Live Here" and "On the Map" the same?

CA **Show What You Know**

Right There
The answer is right there on the page.

READ TOGETHER

The Farmers Market

Many kinds of food grow on a farm. Farmers pick the food when it's ripe.

Trucks take the food to the city. There, it is sold at a farmers market.

Farmers sell fruit, vegetables, and nuts. People come to buy farm-fresh food.

Go on

Directions: Answer the questions.

1 **How do farmers get food to the city?**

A B C

2 **What do farmers do at a farmers market?**

A buy seeds

B sell food

C grow nuts

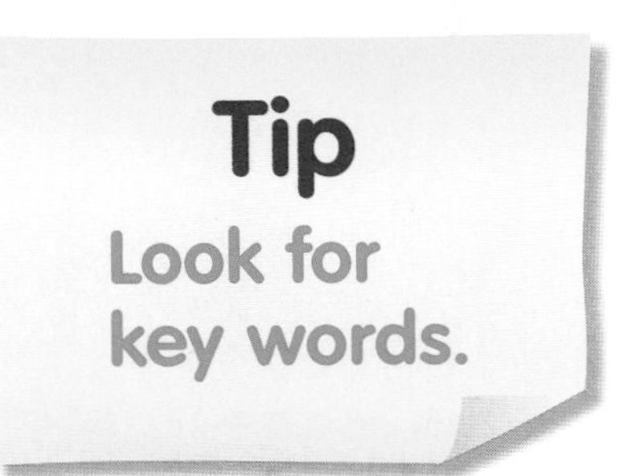

3 **Why is the food at a farmers market special?**

A It comes from other countries.

B It is fresh.

C It is frozen.

Write About Your Neighborhood

Omar wrote about a park.

My block is good for children.

The park has a very big slide.

CA Your Writing Prompt

Think about your neighborhood.

Now write a report telling why your neighborhood is a good place to live.

Writing Hints

 Plan what you will say.

 Use complete sentences.

 Be sure your sentences make sense.

At Home

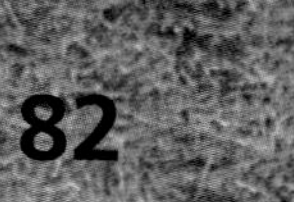

Talk About It

What is a home?

Find out more about homes at www.macmillanmh.com.

Words to Know

again
could
make
one
three
then

Too Big for One

Little Pup is wet **again**.

"We **could make** him a hut," said Pig.
"We could use sticks," said Cat.
"We could use bricks," said Pig.

They used sticks and bricks.
It was a very good hut!

"Is this too big for **one**?" asked Pup.
"It could fit **three**!" said Cat.
Then Pup said, "Come live with me!"
They did.

Comprehension

Genre

A Fantasy is a made-up story that could not really happen.

Story Structure

Plot

Use your Beginning, Middle, and End Chart.

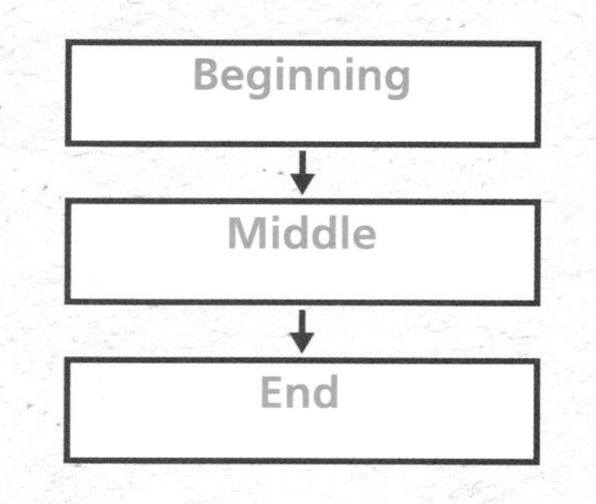

Read to Find Out

What do the pigs do with the mud?

The Pigs, the Wolf, and the Mud

by Ellen Tarlow
illustrated by
Pablo Bernasconi

Three little pigs lived in a mud hut.

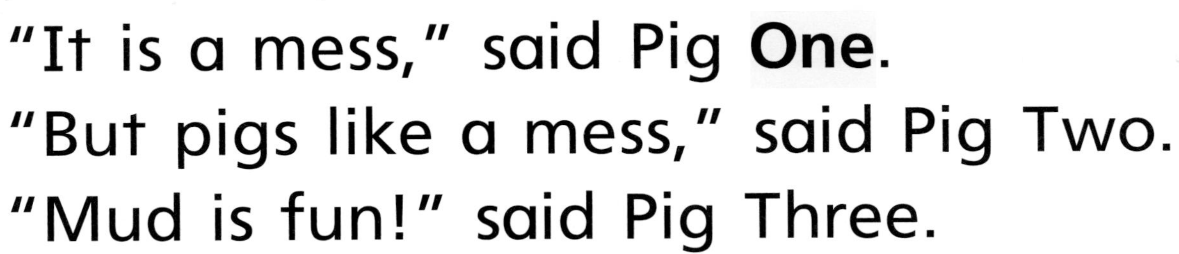

"It is a mess," said Pig **One**.
"But pigs like a mess," said Pig Two.
"Mud is fun!" said Pig Three.

"Get this!" yelled Pig One.
She tossed mud to Pig Two.
"Mud is fun!" yelled Pig Three.

The bell rang.
"Little pigs, little pigs, let me in."

"It is the Big Bad Wolf!" said Pig One. "We can not let you in," yelled the pigs. "You will eat us up."

"**Then** I must huff and puff,"
said the wolf.
He huffed and huffed.
He puffed and puffed.

"Yuck!" said the wolf.
"I can not huff in this dust.
I can not puff in this dust."

The wolf rang the bell **again**.
"Little pigs, let me in!" he yelled.
"We will not let you in!" the pigs
yelled back.

"Then I must kick," said the wolf.
He kicked and kicked.

The hut fell in!
"Yuck!" said the wolf.
"Just look at this mud."

"You pigs are a big mess!"
"Yes!" yelled the pigs.
"Pigs like a big mess!"

"I do not!" yelled the Wolf.
"I must get this mud off.
Good-bye, pigs."

"Let's **make** a hut," said Pig One.
"We **could** use bricks," said Pig Two.
"We could use sticks," said Pig Three.

“Let’s use mud,” said Pig One.
“Mud is best!” said Pig Two.
“Mud is fun!” said Pig Three.
“Yuck!” said the wolf.

Pablo's Place

Pablo Bernasconi loves illustrating animals doing funny things. Pablo's studio is a mess, full of junk and papers. But Pablo loves being surrounded by his things, just as the pigs in the story love being surrounded by mud.

Other books by Pablo Bernasconi

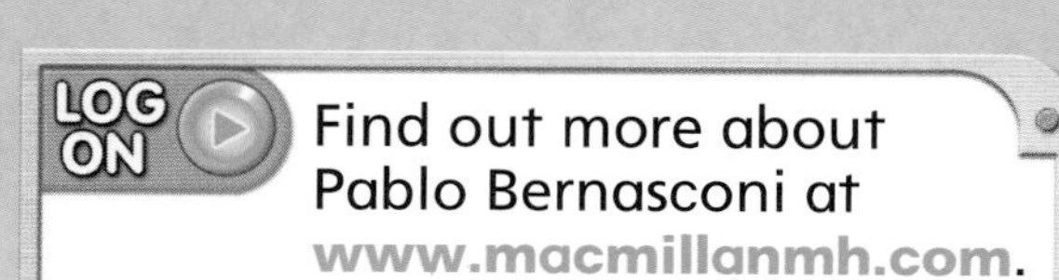

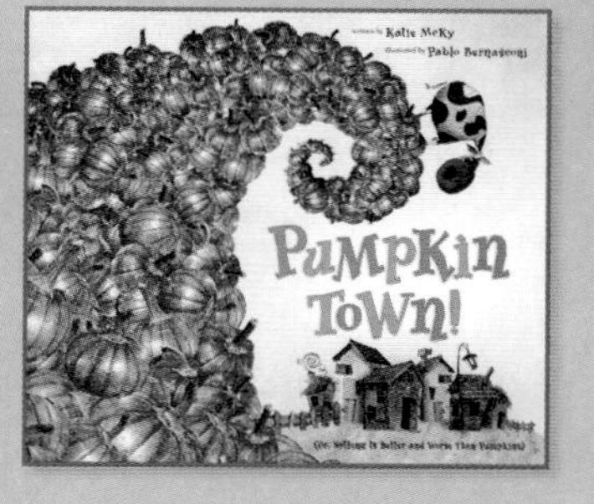

CA Illustrator's Purpose

Pablo Bernasconi loves his messy studio. Draw a place you love being. Write about this place.

Critical Thinking

Retell the Story

Use the Retelling Cards to retell the story in order.

Retelling Cards

Think and Compare

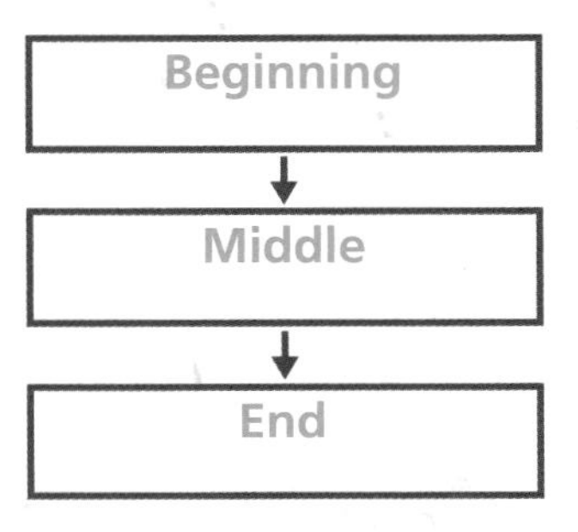

1. What happens when the wolf comes to the pigs' hut?
2. Would you like to live in a mud hut? Why or why not?
3. How are the pigs in this story like real pigs?
4. How are the pigs like Little Pup in "Too Big for One"?

History/
Social Science

Genre
Nonfiction gives information about a topic.

Text Feature
Photographs give more information about the text.

Content Vocabulary
homes
build
shelter

LOG ON Find out more about homes at www.macmillanmh.com.

READ TOGETHER

Homes Around the World

There are many kinds of **homes**. People **build** their homes to fit the place they live.

Look! This home was built into a cliff.

This is a good home for a wet place. There is a lot of water here. The stilts help keep this home dry.

This is a good home for a hot place. There is a lot of clay in this place. People use it to build homes. Clay keeps the home cool inside.

There is a lot of ice in this place. People can use it to build. This is an igloo. Igloos are good **shelter** from the cold.

What is your home like?

CA Critical Thinking

- What kind of home did the pigs live in?
- Why is mud a good home for a pig?

Write About a Funny Animal Home

CA Writing

Proper Nouns

Nouns for special names begin with a capital letter.

Leila wrote about a frog who lived in a tub.

A frog named Ann lived in a tub.

She used soap for her bed!

Your Turn

Think of an animal who lives in a funny home.

Draw a picture.

Write about it.

Writer's Checklist

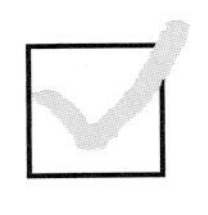 Do I tell where my animal lives?

 Does each special **noun** begin with a capital letter?

 Does my exclamation end with an exclamation mark?

Neighborhood Fun

CA Talk About It

How do the people in your neighborhood have fun together?

LOG ON Find out more about neighborhood fun at **www.macmillanmh.com**.

A Show

Words to Know

- want
- put
- show
- together
- under
- all

Seth and Jill **want** to **put** on a **show**.
They tell lots of kids to come.

The kids want to see the show.
They sit **together under** a tent.

Seth jumps and sings.
Jill spins and taps.
They are very good!

All the kids like the show.
They clap and clap.
"Again!" they yell.

CA Comprehension

Genre

Realistic Fiction is a made-up story that could really happen.

Visualize

Retell

Use your Retelling Chart.

Retelling Chart		
1	→	2
3	→	4
5	→	6

Read to Find Out

What does Beth do with the band?

Beth and the Band

by Anne Miranda
illustrated by Lynne Cravath

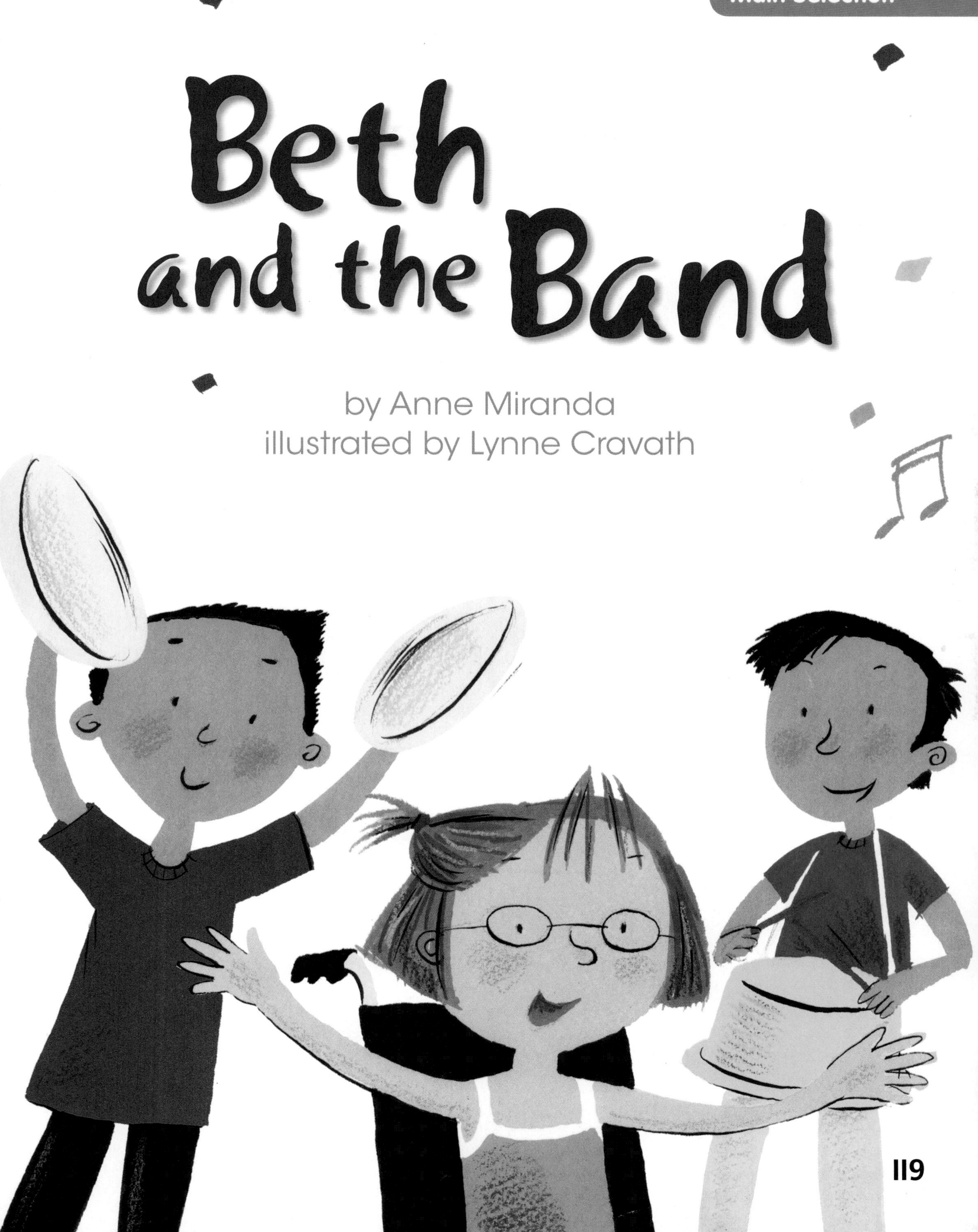

"Aunt Trish, look at that!" said Beth.

"What is it?" asked Aunt Trish.

"It is a band for kids," said Ann.

"We **want** to play in the band!"
said Beth, Bud, Ann, and Will.

"Can the kids **all** play?" asked Aunt Trish.

"Yes!" said a man in a red hat. "I am Shep. Make some instruments, kids."

"Make instruments?" asked the kids.

"Yes. Use the things in the box. It is **under** the bandstand," said Shep.

"I can hit this tub!" said Bud.
"It sounds just like a drum."
Rap! Tap! Tap!

"I can play this jug!" said Ann.
Hum! Hum! Hum!

"I can play the lids!" said Will.
Crish! Crush! Crash!

"What do you want to make, Beth?" asked Aunt Trish.

"I just want to sing," said Beth.

"Can I sing in the **show**?" she asked. "That will be fun for me."

"That will be fun for us, too,"
said the kids.

"Come on," said Will. "Sing with us!"

"Beth and the band will **put** on a show," said Shep.

"Yes!" yelled the kids.

"Let's all play **together**," said Shep.
"One, two, three! Play with me!"

"Jam! Jim! Jam!
Sing with the band!
This fun kids' band
is the best in the land!"

Read Together Sing Along with Anne Miranda

Anne Miranda says, "When I was little, I sang in a group with my friend Elizabeth, her mother, and my neighbor Cathy, who was in high school. Once we were even on TV! We loved making music together, just like Beth and her friends."

Another book by Anne Miranda

LOG ON Find out more about Anne Miranda at **www.macmillanmh.com**.

CA Author's Purpose

Anne Miranda wants to show that friends have fun making music. Draw your friends having fun. Write about it.

Critical Thinking

Retell the Story

Use the Retelling Cards to retell the story in order.

Retelling Cards

Think and Compare

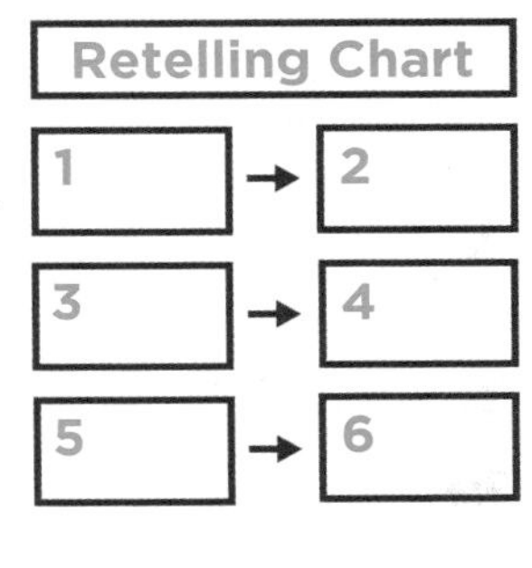

1. What do Beth, Ann, Will, and Bud do at the fair?
2. Would you like to join the kids' band? Tell why or why not.
3. What other instruments do people play in a band?
4. How is the show in this story like the one in "A Show"?

READ TOGETHER

Shake a Rattle!

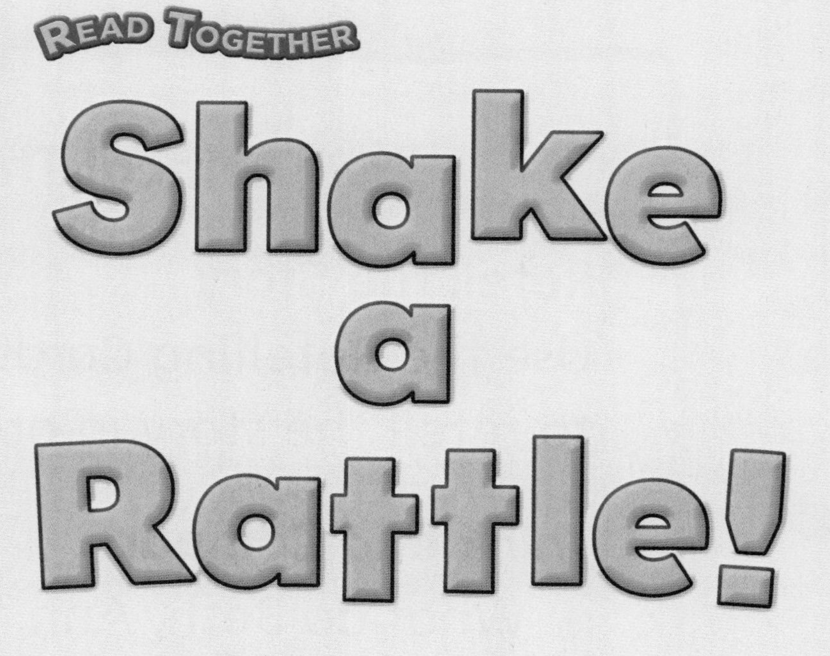

CA **Performing Arts**

Genre

Nonfiction can tell how to do or make something.

Text Feature

Directions are the steps to follow to make something.

Content Vocabulary

instruments

rattles

music

LOG ON Find out more about making music at www.macmillanmh.com.

What **instruments** do you see here? Shaking **rattles** is a fun way to make **music**.

Rattles can be big or little. They can be made of many things. Some have sand in them. Some have beans.

Do you want to make a rattle?
Here's how!

How to Make a Rattle

What You Need

- plastic bottle
- dried beans
- stickers

What to Do

1. Put beans into the bottle.
2. Put fun stickers on.
3. Shake it and have fun!

Can you play the rattle loud? Can you play it soft? Can you make up a song?

Critical Thinking

How is a rattle like the instruments the kids made in *Beth and the Band*?

Writing

Days of the Week

The name of each day begins with a capital letter.

Write About Neighborhood Fun

Leo wrote a story about a fun day.

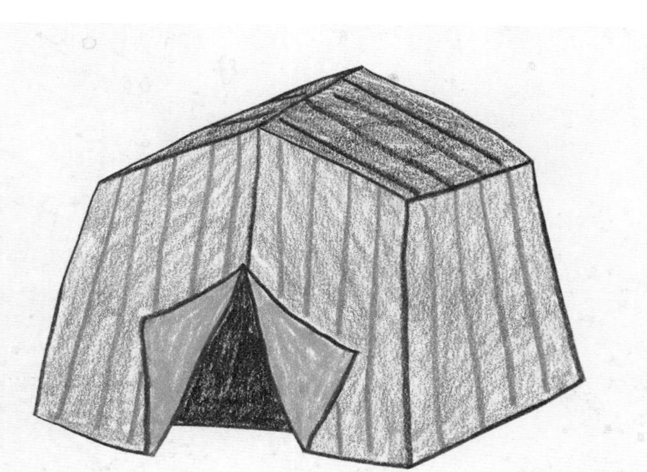

One Saturday, Jim and Ned put up a big tent.

All the kids ate lunch in it.

Your Turn

Think of fun things kids could do in a neighborhood.

Write a story about it.

Name the characters in your story.

Writer's Checklist

Did I write about fun in a neighborhood?

Does my story have characters?

Does the name of each day begin with a capital letter?

Frog Lost

"My frog is lost!" said Gus.

"I will help look," said Meg.

Gus looked under the bed.

Meg looked in her pack.

"What does she like to do?" asked Meg.

"She likes to get wet," said Gus.

Gus and Meg ran to the sink.

Frog sat on a dish, getting a drink!

READ TOGETHER

Make a Book!

What do you see
outside your door?

Show what you see.

Make a book!

front cover

inside pages

back cover

My Book
by
R.A. Cat

The diagram shows
the parts of the book.

What You Need

- one sheet of paper
- crayons

What to Do

Read the directions.

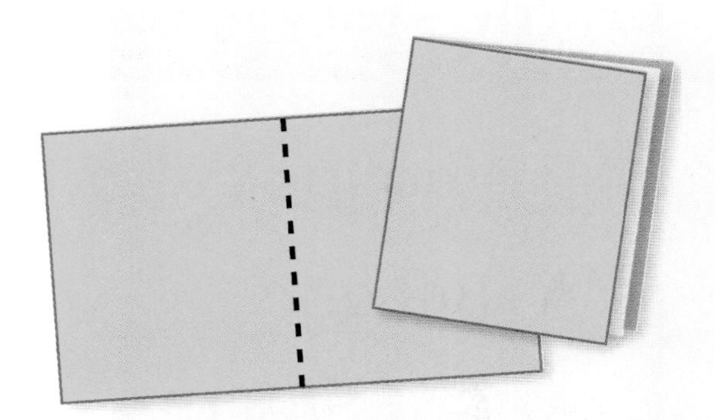

1. Fold your paper.

2. Draw a door on your cover. Write **Outside My Door**.

3. Turn the page. Draw three things outside your door.

4. Write about your pictures.

5. Show your book to a friend!

Critical Thinking

Now answer the questions. Base your answers on the story "Frog Lost."

1 Who looks for Frog?

A Bill and Meg

B Gus and Meg

C Gus

2 Where do they look for Frog?

A in school

B in the yard

C under the bed

3 What happens at the end of the story? Write about it.

Now answer the questions. Base your answers on the story "Make a Book!"

1 What does the diagram show?

A parts of a frog

B parts of a game

C parts of a book

2 What do you need to do to the paper?

A rip it

B cut it

C fold it

Write on Demand

PROMPT Write about something you have made or would like to make. Tell how to make it. Write as much as you can and as well as you can.

Glossary

What Is a Glossary?

A glossary can help you find the meanings of words. The words are listed in alphabetical order. You can look up a word and read it in a sentence. There is a picture to help you.

instrument

place

Sample Entry

Dd

drum

I play the **drum** in the band.

Ee

eat

I like to **eat** dinner with my family.

Hh

hen

A **hen** lays eggs.

Ii

instrument

This **instrument** makes a loud sound.

Jj

jug

The **jug** has milk in it.

Pp

place

The beach is a fun **place**!

Tt

tossed

Ms. Rapp **tossed** the ball to Rosa.

Ww

well

Sam got water from a **well**.

Acknowledgments

The publisher gratefully acknowledges permission to reprint the following copyrighted material:

"Over in the Meadow: An Old Counting Rhyme" by Olive A. Wadsworth. Copyright © 1991 by Scholastic Inc., 730 Broadway, NY, NY. Reprinted with permission of Scholastic Inc., NY.

Book Cover, TO MARKET, TO MARKET by Anne Miranda, illustrated by Janet Stevens. Text copyright © 1997 by Anne Miranda. Illustrations copyright © 1997 by Janet Stevens. Reprinted by permission of Harcourt Children's Books.

Book Cover, ROADRUNNER'S DANCE by Rudolfo Anaya, illustrated by David Diaz. Text copyright © 2000 by Rudolfo Anaya. Illustrations copyright © 2000 by David Diaz. Reprinted by permission of Hyperion Books for Children.

Book Cover, THE LITTLE SCARECROW BOY by Margaret Wise Brown, illustrated by David Diaz. Text copyright © 2005 by Margaret Wise Brown. Illustrations copyright © 2005 by David Diaz. Reprinted by permission of HarperTrophy.

ILLUSTRATIONS

Cover Illustration: Mary Jane Begin

28–33: Krystina Stasiak. 38–41: Anna Vojtech. 42–57: David Diaz. 59-62: Tom Leonard. 71: Mircea Catusanu. 73: Mircea Catusanu. 75–76: Mircea Catusanu. 80: Mike Gordon. 84–87: Marisol Sarrazin. 88–105: Pablo Bernasconi. 110: Ken Bowser. 114–117: Laura Ovresat. 118–135: Lynn Cravath. 140–141: Daniel DelValle. 142–143: Stacy Schuett. 150–153 Brian Karas.

PHOTOGRAPHY

All Photographs are by Ken Cavanagh or Ken Karp for Macmillan/McGraw-Hill (MMH) except as noted below:

Inside front & back covers: The McGraw-Hill Companies/John A. Karachewski, photographer. iv: Steve Bloom. v: Jean-Pierre Lescourret/CORBIS. 2-3: Masterfile Royalty Free. 3: Saxpix/AGE Fotostock. 4: Cathrine Wessel/CORBIS. 5: Stephanie Rausser/CORBIS. 6-7: Steve Bloom Images/Alamy. 8: Anup Shah/Nature Picture Library. 9: Gabriela Staebler/zefa/CORBIS. 10: David A. Northcott/CORBIS. 11: Panthera Productions/Getty Images. 12-13: Steve Bloom. 14: Jean Michel Labat/Ardea London Ltd. 15: Art Wolfe/Photo Researchers. 16: Robert Maier/Animals Animals. 17: Tom & Pat Leeson/Photo Researchers. 18: Michel & Christine Denis-Huot/Photo Researchers. 19: Peter Lilja/Getty Images. 20: Tim Flach/Getty Images. 21: Joe McDonald/CORBIS. 22: Peter Johnson/CORBIS. 23: Inge Yspeert/CORBIS. 24: Steve Bloom. 25: JM Labat/Peter Arnold, Inc. 26: (t) Courtesy Jose Ramos; (b) Art Wolfe/Photo Researchers. 27: Robert Maier/Animals Animals. 34: Peter Beck/CORBIS. 35: Marc Romanelli/Getty Images. 36-37: Ronnie Kaufman/CORBIS. 56: Courtesy of David Diaz. 58-59: (t bkgd) Image 100/Getty Images; (b bkgd) Digital Vision Direct. 59: (c) AGStock USA/Alamy; (cr) C. Borland/PhotoLink/Getty Images. 60: (bkgd) John Prior Images/Alamy. 61: (t bkgd) Image 100/Getty Images; (b bkgd) Digital Vision Direct; (c) JW/Masterfile. 62: (t) Larry Lefever/Grant Heilman Photography; (l) Michael Newman/Photo Edit; (cl) Stock Food/SuperStock. 63: Brand X Pictures/Alamy. 64: Tony Anderson/Getty Images. 65: Michael Newman/Photo Edit. 66-67: Jean-Pierre Lescourret/CORBIS. 68: James Hardy/AGE Fotostock. 69: David Young-Wolff/Alamy. 70: Tony Freeman/Photo Edit. 72: Swerve/Alamy. 74: Andrea Rugg/Beateworks/CORBIS. 76: Bruce Clarke/Index Stock. 78: Jeff Greenburg/Photo Edit. 79: (l to r) Bill Aron/Photo Edit; Rainer Dittrich/Getty Images; Car Culture/Getty Images. 80: LWA-Sharie Kennedy/CORBIS. 81: Bet Noire/Shutterstock. 82-83: Adam Tanner/The Image Works. 104: Courtesy of Natalia Berdini. 106: Mediacolor's/Alamy. 107: Upperhall Ltd./Robert Harding World Imagery/CORBIS. 108: Stone/Getty Images. 109: Bryan & Cherry Alexander Photography. 110: Roy Morsch/AGE Fotostock. 111: Design Pics Inc/Alamy. 112-113: Cwener Photography/Index Stock Imagery. 134: Courtesy Anne Miranda. 136: (cr) Canadian Museum of Civilization/CORBIS; (bl) David Young-Wolff/Photo Edit; (bc) allOver photography/Alamy; (br) Royalty-Free/CORBIS. 137: (c) AP Photo/Pat Vasquez-Cunningham; (br) Dynamic Graphics Group/Creatas/Alamy. 140: David Schmidt/Masterfile. 144: Thinkstock/Getty Images. 145: Stockdisc/PunchStock. 148: (cr) C Squared Studios/Getty Images; (bl) Jeff Zaruba/CORBIS. 149: (t) Robert Maier/Animals Animals; (b) Bananastock/Alamy. 150: Ariel Skelley/CORBIS. 151: (t) Robert Maier/Animals Animals; (b) C Squared Studios/Getty Images. 152: Jeff Zaruba/CORBIS. 153: Bananastock/Alamy. CA Standards pages 1-4: Medioimages/PunchStock.

Reading/Language Arts
CA California Standards
Grade 1

READING

1.0 Word Analysis, Fluency, and Systematic Vocabulary Development
Students understand the basic features of reading. They select letter patterns and know how to translate them into spoken language by using phonics, syllabication, and word parts. They apply this knowledge to achieve fluent oral and silent reading.

Concepts About Print

1.1	Match oral words to printed words.
1.2	Identify the title and author of a reading selection.
1.3	Identify letters, words, and sentences.

Phonemic Awareness

1.4	Distinguish initial, medial, and final sounds in single-syllable words.
1.5	Distinguish long-and short-vowel sounds in orally stated single-syllable words (e.g., *bit/bite*).
1.6	Create and state a series of rhyming words, including consonant blends.
1.7	Add, delete, or change target sounds to change words (e.g., change *cow* to *how; pan* to *an).*
1.8	Blend two to four phonemes into recognizable words (e.g., */c/ a/ t/* = cat; */f/ l/ a/ t/* = flat).
1.9	Segment single-syllable words into their components (e.g., */c/ a/ t/* = cat; */s/ p/ l/ a/ t/* = splat; */r/ i/ ch/* = rich).

Decoding and Word Recognition

1.10	Generate the sounds from all the letters and letter patterns, including consonant blends and long-and short-vowel patterns (i.e., phonograms), and blend those sounds into recognizable words.
1.11	Read common, irregular sight words (e.g., *the, have, said, come, give, of).*
1.12	Use knowledge of vowel digraphs and *r-* controlled letter-sound associations to read words.
1.13	Read compound words and contractions.
1.14	Read inflectional forms (e.g., *-s, -ed, -ing)* and root words (e.g., *look, looked, looking).*
1.15	Read common word families (e.g., *-ite, -ate).*
1.16	Read aloud with fluency in a manner that sounds like natural speech.

Vocabulary and Concept Development

1.17 Classify grade-appropriate categories of words (e.g., concrete collections of animals, foods, toys).

2.0 **Reading Comprehension**
Students read and understand grade-level-appropriate material. They draw upon a variety of comprehension strategies as needed (e.g., generating and responding to essential questions, making predictions, comparing information from several sources). The selections in *Recommended Literature, Kindergarten Through Grade Twelve* illustrate the quality and complexity of the materials to be read by students. In addition to their regular school reading, by grade four, students read one-half million words annually, including a good representation of grade-level-appropriate narrative and expository text (e.g., classic and contemporary literature, magazines, newspapers, online information). In grade one, students begin to make progress toward this goal.

Structural Features of Informational Materials

2.1 Identify text that uses sequence or other logical order.

Comprehension and Analysis of Grade-Level-Appropriate Text

2.2 Respond to *who, what, when, where,* and *how* questions.

2.3 Follow one-step written instructions.

2.4 Use context to resolve ambiguities about word and sentence meanings.

2.5 Confirm predictions about what will happen next in a text by identifying key words (i.e., signpost words).

2.6 Relate prior knowledge to textual information.

2.7 Retell the central ideas of simple expository or narrative passages.

3.0 **Literary Response and Analysis** Students read and respond to a wide variety of significant works of children's literature. They distinguish between the structural features of the text and the literary terms or elements (e.g., theme, plot, setting, characters). The selections in *Recommended Literature, Kindergarten Through Grade Twelve* illustrate the quality and complexity of the materials to be read by students.

Narrative Analysis of Grade-Level-Appropriate Text

3.1 Identify and describe the elements of plot, setting, and character(s) in a story, as well as the story's beginning, middle, and ending.

3.2 Describe the roles of authors and illustrators and their contributions to print materials.

3.3 Recollect, talk, and write about books read during the school year.

WRITING

1.0 **Writing Strategies** Students write clear and coherent sentences and paragraphs that develop a central idea. Their writing shows they consider the audience and purpose. Students progress through the stages of the writing process (e.g., prewriting, drafting, revising, editing successive versions).

Organization and Focus

1.1 Select a focus when writing.

1.2 Use descriptive words when writing.

Penmanship

1.3 Print legibly and space letters, words, and sentences appropriately.

2.0 **Writing Applications (Genres and Their Characteristics)** Students write compositions that describe and explain familiar objects, events, and experiences. Student writing demonstrates a command of standard American English and the drafting, research, and organizational strategies outlined in Writing Standard 1.0.
Using the writing strategies of grade one outlined in Writing Standard 1.0, students:

2.1 Write brief narratives (e.g., fictional, autobiographical) describing an experience.

2.2 Write brief expository descriptions of a real object, person, place, or event, using sensory details.

WRITTEN AND ORAL ENGLISH LANGUAGE CONVENTIONS

The standards for written and oral English language conventions have been placed between those for writing and for listening and speaking because these conventions are essential to both sets of skills.

1.0 **Written and Oral English Language Conventions** Students write and speak with a command of standard English conventions appropriate to this grade level.

Sentence Structure

1.1 Write and speak in complete, coherent sentences.

Grammar

1.2 Identify and correctly use singular and plural nouns.

1.3 Identify and correctly use contractions (e.g., *isn't, aren't, can't, won't)* and singular possessive pronouns (e.g., *my/ mine, his/ her, hers, your/s)* in writing and speaking.

Punctuation	
1.4	Distinguish between declarative, exclamatory, and interrogative sentences.
1.5	Use a period, exclamation point, or question mark at the end of sentences.
1.6	Use knowledge of the basic rules of punctuation and capitalization when writing.
Capitalization	
1.7	Capitalize the first word of a sentence, names of people, and the pronoun *I*.
Spelling	
1.8	Spell three-and four-letter short-vowel words and grade-level-appropriate sight words correctly.

LISTENING AND SPEAKING

1.0 **Listening and Speaking Strategies** Students listen critically and respond appropriately to oral communication. They speak in a manner that guides the listener to understand important ideas by using proper phrasing, pitch, and modulation.

Comprehension	
1.1	Listen attentively.
1.2	Ask questions for clarification and understanding.
1.3	Give, restate, and follow simple two-step directions.
Organization and Delivery of Oral Communication	
1.4	Stay on the topic when speaking.
1.5	Use descriptive words when speaking about people, places, things, and events.

2.0 **Speaking Applications (Genres and Their Characteristics)** Students deliver brief recitations and oral presentations about familiar experiences or interests that are organized around a coherent thesis statement. Student speaking demonstrates a command of standard American English and the organizational and delivery strategies outlined in Listening and Speaking Standard 1.0.

Using the speaking strategies of grade one outlined in Listening and Speaking Standard 1.0, students:

2.1	Recite poems, rhymes, songs, and stories.
2.2	Retell stories using basic story grammar and relating the sequence of story events by answering *who, what, when, where, why,* and *how* questions.
2.3	Relate an important life event or personal experience in a simple sequence.
2.4	Provide descriptions with careful attention to sensory detail.